The Most Terrifying Places on Earth

Searching Through the World's Most Horrifying and Scary Locations

Conrad Bauer

Disclaimer

Copyrights

Disclaimer and Terms of Use

MAPLEWOOD PUBLISHING

Contents

Introduction

The world around us is a scary place. With danger lurking around so many corners, the threats we can explain are often easily quantified and dismissed. Rather, it is the unexplainable, the paranormal and the strange, that present the biggest threats to our psychological well-being. All across the planet, certain places have come to represent these abnormal and unexplainable phenomena. From ghosts to genocides, brutal murders to witches' covens, these locations can be both hyper-specific and universal.

In almost every town, village, and city, there is often an area where people are wary. A certain building people say is haunted, or a home they know has a particularly gruesome past. Adults might warn children to stay away, these buildings might form the backbone of some local folklore, or they might actually be condemned and restricted to the public. In these buildings, our imaginations run riot. We wonder what could be possibly be lurking down the long, dank, dark corridors. However, not all of these places are created equal.

In this book, we will examine some of the most terrifying, strange, bizarre, odd, and depressing places on earth. These might be haunted homes or the resting place of a murderous maniac. Some have been created by the evils of modern man while others are tributes to ancient and dark mysteries we still struggle to explain. The one thing they share is their ability to chill you to the bone. As you work through this list, the true extent of humanity's capacity to imagine the horrific should not be underestimated. When you are ready to learn about some of the worst places in the world, read on.

The Island of the Dolls, Mexico

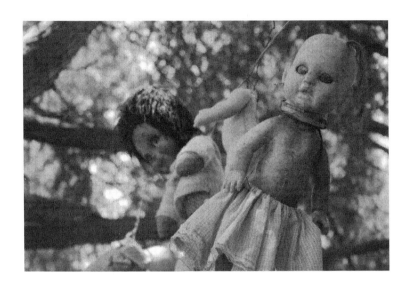

We begin our journey with a trip to Mexico. Found nestled along the canals of Xochimico and on the outskirts of Mexico City, one of the world's oddest locations has become something of a tourist destination. Though it was never designed to be an attraction, Mexico's Island of the Dolls is becoming one of the key destinations for those visiting the city in search of the strange. However, it began life as a tribute to a departed little girl, taken from this world too soon.

Known locally as Isla de las Munecas, the island is located to the south of the Mexican capital city. Its key defining feature is the presence of hundreds, possibly thousands, of mutilated children's toys. These dolls litter the surroundings, their severed limbs, removed heads, torn limbs, and lifeless eyes staring down every person who dares approach. They are scattered and hung across fences, trees, and buildings. Wherever there is an available surface, a strangled doll sits, scolding onlookers. Though their presence is strange enough during the day, it is when the sun sets that their inhumanity and potential to terrify really takes over.

Where do these dolls come from? As mentioned above, the story is a tragic one. The tale begins close to half a century ago, when the man who was the island's sole inhabitant discovered the body of a child who had drowned in the canal. Don Julian Santana was shaken by the death and the discovery of the corpse. So much so that, when he later saw a doll drift by the same location, he reached out and removed it from the river. Not knowing where it had come from or why it had arrived, he hung it from a tree as a tribute to the drowned girl of the canal. He wanted to help settle her restless soul, as well as to provide some degree of protection for his island.

But the single doll in the tree was not enough. Don Santana was increasingly uneasy. As the days went by, he began to notice more and more doll parts floating down past the island. Each time he would see a plastic face journeying along, Santana reached into the water and plucked it out. He would hang the doll (or a discarded body part) somewhere on the island. But there were never enough. Soon, he moved beyond the confines of the island and began to search through local scrap heaps and rubbish piles. He foraged for dolls wherever he could find them, taking these parts back to his island to arrange them as he saw fit. He even began to trade the food he grew to feed himself in exchange for more plastic figures. Every time a new doll came to the island, he would carefully select a place and arrange the arrival in a designated spot.

Over the coming years, his deeds would become infamous in the local community. People soon began to tell stories about the Island of the Dolls. They would say Don Santana was a mad man, a deranged maniac who believed the dolls to be his own children, children he had rescued from the river and tried to save from drowning. As with all local folk tales, there was little truth in this version of events.

Today, the island is owned by Don Santana's family. They hold the insight into the reasoning behind its creation. For them, the suggestion is that the creator truly believed the soul of the original girl haunted the island. Each addition of a doll was designed to placate her spirit. To make her happy and to try and keep the threat of evil at a safe distance, Santana's careful placement of discarded plastic children was intended to ward away negative spirits.

The dolls were not able to protect Don Santana himself. In 2001, he fell into the canal himself and drowned, just like the little girl whose memory haunted him for decades. The locals, buoyed by this development, began to suggest the dolls might have turned on their creator. Others have suggested that, in the absence of the island's protector, the dolls themselves have taken on the duty to watch over the soul of anyone who might stand there.

Ever since the death of Don Santana, the island has received an increased amount of attention. Now run by his family as a tourist attraction, it has been visited by many journalists and film crews who hope to gain that little bit of insight into the life of the creator of the Island of the Dolls. For those who are arriving at the island, perhaps the scariest part is the path to get there. The route to Don Santana's creation is littered with the discarded limbs of those dolls who were not deemed worthy of protecting the island. These sun-bleached and broken figures have now provided homes to spiders, bugs and snakes, meaning that a simple walk to an already scary place is now beset by a plastic wasteland of little limbs and cracked eyes, crawled over by many people's worst nightmares. As if the Island of the Dolls was not terrifying enough, those trying to reach Don Santana's legacy must first pass through the wasteland of ruined toys and creepy crawlies.

Hashima Island, Japan

The next stop in our journey will take us from an island of tiny plastic faces to a veritable ghost town. Rather than being a town filled with the undead and spirits, however, Hashima Island in Japan is a stark reminder of how worrying a lack of humanity can become. Travelling to the location involves departing from a port in Nagasaki, one of only two locations in the world attacked using nuclear weapons. Those who have made the journey report the strange serenity as the ship moves out from the harbour and into the choppy waters. Occasional storms and biting waves attack the hull of the boats as interested parties move towards one of the Far East's strangest abandoned cities.

At just over the size of a dozen football pitches, Hashima is the official name for this speck of land. For those interested in a translation, the name Battleship Island might be the closest we can get. Anyone who has ever viewed the silhouette of the island at night, outlined against a setting sun, will immediately recognise the imposing shadow of a dreadnought rising from the horizon. Up until the mid-seventies, it was used as a facility for mining. After this, humanity left the concrete city alone. Left to the threat of the ocean elements, the concrete buildings have spent thirty years being tossed and turned against any weather the sea can muster.

What has been left is a skeleton city. The silence of the island is juxtaposed against the typical sights and sounds one expects to hear when standing among the concrete towers. Where we might normally hear laughter, footsteps, or the simple buzz of electricity, instead there is only the distant lap of waves against the stone walls of the island constructs. Where the place once hummed with the business of a Japanese mining community, visitors to the island now report the strange and horrifying silence. It's apocalyptic, uneasy, and unerring.

The island has had some claims to fame in recent years. It was briefly opened for tourists in 2009 and still welcomes journalists and photographers who wish to look into the contrast between the industrialized future and the reclaimed rocks. There has even been a film crew visiting, with part of the James Bond film Skyfall shot on location. As the villain's secret lair, the empty windows and abandoned homes provide a bedrock of evil from which he launched his devious plans.

But if it is simply an old set of homes, why has this island been included in this list of terrifying locations? Without visiting the location, it is hard to convey the sense of feral dread housed within the empty walls. Even before the sun sets, those who are "lucky" enough to make it past the crashing waves and up the rusting gantries will be able to wander through the deserted streets. With each footstep, the echoes of silence ring around the entire island. Each step is a crashing reminder of the isolation of the individual and the fragile nature of humanity's most powerful structures.

The ease with which nature has risen up and over the imposing concrete superstructure is enough to remind any person about their own mortality. After taking so long to create and providing such an industrial function, the casual reclamation of Hashima following the departure of its residents is a telling reminder of just how close we can be to returning to the dust and the dirt. With the distant lingering atomic dread in the background, anyone who has ever wondered what the world might be like should we all perish need only take a few steps along Battleship Island.

Simply put, Hashima is a dead place. It was abandoned and left to rot. Where families once spent their days, rust and dust have crawled up from the ground. After just a few steps through the town, you will never want to be alone again. For pure, industrial dread that is hard to find anywhere else in the world, a trip to Hashima is all that is required.

The Hill of Crosses, Lithuania

From the abandoned industrial island, our attention now turns towards something with more of an ancient concern. Despite the cross's importance to Christianity, the presence of a crucifix is still a timely reminder of death and as an instrument of torture. The Romans would nail people to these pieces of intersected wood when they wished them a particularly painful death. This was the fate said to have befallen Jesus Christ, and over the millennia since his death, the cross has become a sign of veneration and religiosity. While a single cross might be a reminder of faith, a hill crowded with such items can be incredibly horrific. In Lithuania, the Hill of the Crosses is exactly that.

Found twelve kilometers north of the city of Šiauliai, the hill has a muddied past. No one can trace the beginning of the practice of placing numerous crosses at this particular place. However, some have traced the lineage back to the ruins of a hill fort at the location, destroyed during the local uprising of 1831. Ever since, people have been adding crosses every day. Not only small and manageable examples, but also giant crucifixes that dominate the landscape. As well as the crosses, statues and carvings of saints and folk heroes have been added. Images of the Virgin Mary are included, and thousands of rosaries, tributes, and effigies have been laid at the site. The most recent estimates have suggested there could be as many as one hundred thousand crosses at the site.

As one glimpse at the attached image will tell you, it does not take much for a simple show of faith to turn into a looming, threatening landscape. As you step up towards the hill, these instruments of death and reminders of Catholicism rear up over the top of the hill. Reaching up like fingers from the earth, there is barely an inch of ground visible among the row upon row of crosses. If the saying goes that a person might not be able to see a forest for the trees, the chances of seeing anything other than thousands of spikey, gnarled crosses is incredibly low.

As well as an eerie symbol of death, the cross graveyard has come to signify the enduring qualities of the country's Catholic population. Having been victimized across countless centuries and subjugated during numerous wars, Lithuania's accumulation of crosses at the site is not only a reminder of the sacrifice of the believer's God, but also of the sacrifice of their ancestors. Unsuccessful rebellions against the Russians in 1831 and 1863 are just two examples of times when the local population has been decimated by the overlords who controlled the territory. With families unable to locate the bodies of those put to death, the addition of the crosses to the hill is one explanation for the sheer expansion of the Hill of Crosses over the centuries.

In addition to remembering the dead, the site has also been used as a place for Lithuanians to pray on current circumstances. During the European upheaval of 1918 – the First World War and the Bolshevik Revolution – the country's claims to independence were often met with bloodshed and terror. During later Soviet occupation, the Hill's importance as a traditional source of Lithuanian national identity helped citizens endure decades of foreign rule. It became the site for numerous peaceful protests as well as violent demonstrations. Because of this, the Soviets worked to remove the additional crosses as they began to pile up on the site.

However, after the fall of the USSR and the forging of an independent local government, the Hill of the Crosses only swelled in size. Nowadays, through sun and snow, the huge volume of stark shapes looms up out of the ground. As well as a religious figure, each cross has come to represent those who lost their lives during a tumultuous time for the country. Because of this, the curious nature of the site has become something of a graveyard. With tombstones often being enough to stir ill feeling in many people, the prospect of spending a night between the hundreds of thousands of dark crosses and the dead they represent might be too spooky for some. Eerily still, Lithuania's Hill of Crosses is a site of quiet and serene terror.

Aokigahara, Japan

Throughout this book, there are a number of places that have witnessed great atrocities and horrible murders. Others simply seem as though they are cursed. Those who pass through these places have noted the sense of dread and fear that overcomes them, despite nothing noticeable in the area. Even some areas of immense natural beauty can come under this banner. One such location is Aokigahara in Japan, commonly referred to as both the Sea of Trees and the Suicide Forest.

Located near the base of Japan's Mount Fuji, the iconic backdrop does nothing to prevent the place becoming one of the most dreaded in all of the world. With many believing it is the home of numerous broken souls, demons, and the lost dead, it had become famous throughout the country and the planet for the effect it has on people.

To the northwest of the famous mountain, the peak appears over the top of the trees and looms over the wooden area. While many other views of the mountain are remarked upon for their beauty, the fourteen square miles of forest known as Aokigahara might appear – from a distance – as an extension of this serene natural vista. As you might have come to expect, however, appearances can often be very deceiving.

For first-time visitors to Aokigahara, there is an immediate sensation that something is not quite right. Call it intuition or the ability to tune into the paranormal, but visitors to the area have reported noticing the difference in ambiance straight away. There is a silence pervading the area. The trees are packed together tightly, presented as a dense wooden wall to the surrounding world. You are isolated, alone, and placed inside a small world of your own. While you might expect to hear birds and other wildlife, all forms of life appear to have abandoned the area. They can often be heard in the distance, almost as a warning to anyone who enters the forest.

Another strange feature of the area is a particular problem for walkers, hikers, or anyone who is lost. Compasses behave very strangely in the vicinity of Aokigahara, refusing to align with the correct directions. Scientists have traced this issue to a large amount of iron deposits in the soil, their magnetism interfering with travelers' attempts to navigate the forest with any degree of accuracy. With the dense vista of trees hiding any external points of reference, it is easy to get lost amongst the trees. To get around this issue, visitors often leave behind plastic markers or traces designed to provide them a lifeline to the outside world.

These markers add to the strange litter left on the forest floor. For many, these strange items are the first really odd element of the area. Those who walk among the trees will often find pairs of discarded shoes on the ground. These come in adult and children's sizes, some arranged in a neat and tidy manner, others strewn around the floor, aged and covered in moss. Some of the shoes have been there for an incredible amount of time and are steadily crumbling into the forest themselves. Coupled with this phenomena, toys and dolls are left lying around or placed into the branches of quiet trees. The cold, dead eyes stare out. All through the forest, the children's small toys and trinkets present a clue into the world of people who once passed through the area

To say the area is abandoned would be a lie. There are a steady stream of visitors to the forest, due in part to the outstanding natural beauty of the surrounding area and the reputation Aokigahara has built up. There are signs placed around the area to warn visitors of the large craggy caverns they could fall into as well as the world of empty tunnels and caves that twist and turn beneath the mossy ground.

But apart from the visitors and the strange items littered around the forest floor, there is a more sinister element to the fame of Aokigahara. As you might have guessed already, the area is thought to be the final resting place of hundreds, possibly thousands, of people who have journeyed here to die.

Aokigahara has been given the morbid tagline of "the perfect place to die," almost like a paranormal travel agency has tried to promote the location. With the natural beauty and the quietness inherent to the area, there are certainly worse final resting places. Throughout the world, it is difficult to find a more popular suicide spot than the Aokigahara forest. For the previous half century, the area's reputation has been growing, with ever-increasing numbers of suicidal people travelling to the location to end their lives. There are specially appointed guards who travel through the woods once a month to find and remove the bodies. Once a year, a volunteer task force moves through the area on a "body hunt" to track down the corpses that the guards might have missed. The only thing they do not remove are the victims' shoes.

Even estimates of the correct number of annual suicides are thought to be conservative. With so many remote and distant parts of Aokigahara, discovering all of the bodies is almost impossible. With the myriad caverns, nooks, and crannies, the huge number of potential places for people to take their own lives is huge. Hikers who travel through the area have sometimes looked up from their dancing compass to be greeted by a pair of feet belonging to a despondent person who has hanged themselves from a tree. The only fact the authorities can know for sure is that the number of suicides in the area seems to be on the increase.

For those who guard the area, three types of visitor have been noticed. While on guard, they typically enter visitors into one of these three groups. First, there are the hikers who have come to get a glimpse of the beautiful geography in the area, such as the trees and the sights of Mount Fuji. Second, there are those who have learned about the reputation the area has built up and have come to visit because of this morbid curiosity or desire to help. The last group are those who have travelled to Aokigahara to end their lives. To combat the efforts of the final group, authorities have begun to erect a series of signs around the forest, imploring visitors not to end their lives. They have even set up a network of closed circuit television cameras to monitor the forest and report on anyone who might be in need of help. Despite this, around one hundred people every year commit suicide in the forest, a rate of almost two every week.

For some, it is the pull of the forest that draws doomed souls towards Aokigahara. Folklore says that paranormal forces send out a signal to the suicidal, encouraging them to travel to the forest. Once they have arrived, their final thoughts are embellished by the swirling negativity, and they are encouraged to end it all. Those who have survived suicide attempts in the area have recalled a certain feeling of being drawn towards Aokigahara and being compelled to travel to the forest, regardless of where they might be.

The phenomena is not exclusively modern. For centuries, Aokigahara has held a place in local folklore as being a focus of negative, devilish, and malicious spirits. These have attacked, terrified, and worried travelers for hundreds of years. Some have suggested the area is filled with ghosts and demons who prey on the unsuspecting and the unaware. There are even reports that Aokigahara was once the site for people to practice the maligned tradition of ubasute, wherein the old and frail are taken to a remote location and left to die, an ancient form of euthanasia. Folklore dictates that these elderly dead would become vengeful spirits, exerting their wrath on those who came to the area.

For modern investigators, it is often suggested that the trees themselves have absorbed the negativity that surrounds the numerous suicides. With so much death and tragedy nearby, these growing, living plants have drawn up the maliciousness through their roots and broadcast it almost like a radio signal. This broadcast reaches out to those in a delicate or dark position and becomes a suggestive encouragement to add their own name to the increasing list of victims.

Those who have conducted investigations into the haunted forest of Aokigahara have found that there is often no one, uniting motivation among those attempting suicide in the area. The one common factor uniting them all is the strange pull exerted on them by the trees and the ground in this location. For a group united by their intention to end their own lives, an area which is seemingly overflowing with beauty has become a final ending place for those driven by an overriding suicidal compulsion. At the foot of Japan's most famous mountain lies one of the world's most horror-inducing places. If you ever find yourself in the shadow of Mount Fuji and your compass begins to dance, remember to veer away from the darkest of thoughts, and be careful not to trip over the shoes of those who visited before you.

Paris Catacombs, France

It is often supposed that the world's most terrifying places are limited to isolated places, single buildings or at least somewhere we can be certain to avoid. For our next entry, however, the terror lurks beneath one of the world's most famous cities. Beneath Paris, the catacombs are twisted corridors lined with the bones of the dead. Holding the last known remains of close to six million people, the ossuaries are essentially a series of interconnected caves, tunnels, corridors, and caverns. If the prospect of the dead and the dying is one that might be deemed fear-inducing, the catacombs of Paris are one of the world's scariest locations.

Having now earned the title as the "World's Largest Grave," it dates back hundreds of years and is one that people may walk through. The catacombs began life as a series of stone mines located to the south of the city's ancient southern gate. Over the course of the last two hundred years, their availability to the public has often changed, with authorities allowing entrants to the graves periodically and closing them just as regularly. As of December 19, 2009, the catacombs were open to public examination. As such, they are included as one of Paris's fourteen great museums, their importance placed alongside the Louvre as an insight into France's past. Actually a series interconnected graves, the name "the catacombs" refers both to one specific area and the network as a whole.

The earliest parts of the burial network began on what was once the southern outskirts of the Roman city known as Left Bank. After the collapse of Roman rule in the area and the invasion of the Franks, the citizenry of the area were left without much in the way of rule and began to leave the area. One of the few buildings that remained was a fourth century church and its attached burial grounds. Around this, urban expansions were erected, and what we know as the modern city of Paris began to spring up in the surrounding area. While cultures in other cities would bury their dead far from the population, Parisians from this time and in the ensuing centuries placed their cemeteries and graves right in the heart of the city.

Of all the graves found in the ancient town, one of the most famous would become the one attached to the Saints Innocents church. Throughout the first millennium, while wars raged around France, the church would rise in importance to become one of Paris's most important religious institutions and its primary cemetery. But as the city expanded, the numbers of dead began to increase. Soon, the limited space available in churches was becoming sparse. Finding room to bury the dead was a growing concern. Not only did mourners wish to pay their respects, but the proximity with rotting bodies was certainly a concern. In order to clear space and find fresh room for the newly deceased, older bodies were exhumed and taken from their traditional resting places. They were used to line the walls of the various cemetery grounds and tunnels in the city. By the time the nineteenth century began, these walls of bones and skulls had reached two meters high. Thanks to wars, famines, diseases, plagues, fires, and the slow march of death, the numbers of bones rose and rose. Conditions in the cemeteries were bad, but the creation of these catacombs provided an outlet for the huge amount of human remains that came with a growing city.

After a series of political mandates limited the use of inner-city cemeteries, the decision was reached to create a number of larger scale solutions. Following on from a process begun in the eighteenth century, Parisians began to move all of the dead into grounds on the outer reaches of the city, condemning the church cemeteries that existed within the limits of Paris.

The history of the catacombs is inextricably linked to the abandoned mines that built much of Paris. Thanks to the ancient mining techniques, tunnels and corridors would often be left unmapped and abandoned if they proved to be drained of resources. As these were often uncharted and even illegal, and as the city spread outwards and incorporated the mines into the city limits, they lay underneath the swelling city, often without those above realizing it. As these mines began to collapse when the buildings above grew too heavy, it was decided that the problems of the dead and the mines could be combined.

As the cemeteries closed and the piles of bones grew, collapsing buildings became more frequent. The mines were bolstered and consolidated. People would travel through the abandoned shafts and map them out. Underground and without the right lighting and the right support, the potential for dead ends, sudden collapses, and strange sights and sounds were plentiful. Nevertheless, in 1785, the government took the decision to eradicate both of their problems and to move the remains of the dead into the collapsing tunnels. Just as the bones had bolstered the walls of the cemeteries, they were used to line the abandoned passageways of the unused and increasingly dangerous mines.

The process of moving bones into the mines was not taken lightly. Affectations and decorations from the filled cemeteries were used to create the right ambiance among the dead. The head of the project, Louis-Étienne Héricart de Thury, did not arrange the bones and skulls in order of time or location of death. Instead, femurs were stacked on femurs, skulls placed next to skulls. There was something of a grim decoration process, with the arrangements decided upon for maximum artistic merit and maximum aesthetic impact. It it should be no surprise when people who travel through the catacombs realised the weight of the city's death as it surrounds them.

There is even a room dedicated solely to the skeletal abnormalities and estrangements found among the dead. Coupled with the morbid inscriptions and poetic messages left in the corridors, visitors recall being literally surrounded by a strong specter of death.

While other locations may need to be embellished by the paranormal and the strange, the terror of the Parisian catacombs is apparent from the start. Found underneath the city, the walls are lined with the bones of the dead, propping up the tunnels to prevent them from collapsing. For anyone who wants to know the price of growing a capital, the dead support the city of Paris in a very literal sense. As well as the sense of history, the authenticity of the skeletons and skulls lining the catacombs adds to the strange and perhaps wonderful sensation offered by these terrifying tunnels.

Pripyat, Ukraine

If the piles of human bones or the suicide forest seems unappealing enough, then there are certain places in the world that combine terror, quietness, and actual harm. As a species, humanity has developed the means to destroy itself many times over. One of the lasting legacies to this destructive power can be found in Ukraine. While not the victim of a nuclear attack, the meltdown that occurred at Chernobyl has rendered a huge swathe of land uninhabitable. For the once prosperous town of Pripyat, this has resulted in a radioactive ghost town.

Nearly thirty years after the events in the Ukrainian power station, the threat of radioactivity still lingers in the area. Despite this, carefully controlled visits to Pripyat are growing in popularity. The accident occurred in 1986, when the core of a local nuclear reactor was being tested to determine its limits. Nominally a regular testing process, a series of unfortunate accidents led to a huge explosion. The resulting meltdown contaminated a huge area, including Pripyat, spreading all across Europe in varying degrees. While initial death tolls were seemingly limited to just thirty people, several thousand more may have perished due to the resulting radioactive contamination.

The nearby town – and the subject of this entry – was Pripyat. With a population of nearly fifty thousand at the time of the accident, it had originally been founded to house the employees of the nuclear reactor. Situated just three kilometers from the reactor, it was evacuated immediately and still contains traces of the explosion. Now abandoned, the town stands as a tribute to the potential threat of nuclear war. The whole of Pirpyat is now a lasting reminder of what might happen should the worst fears of a nuclear winter come to pass.

This has left the town as something of a frozen image. There are still hanging posters proclaiming the benefits of the communist party, long after the fall of the Soviets. The town itself is covered in decorations, preparing for a local holiday set to take place days after the explosion. Toys are left on the floor and work lies uncompleted on the desks of a school. Every single clock is left standing at the same time – five minutes to noon. This was the time the electricity was cut to the town, noting its official abandonment.

In the place of humanity, the local wildlife has thrived. Plants, rats, foxes, lynx, elk, and birds have all been spotted in the contaminated zone. As much as they seem to thrive, however, they remain at a hugely increased risk of cancer. Animals wander into Pripyat and enjoy a fruitful but ultimately doomed existence. There have even been reports of plants that glow in the dark. It might say something that the thriving wildlife of Pripyat benefits more from the fallout of a nuclear meltdown than they do from the presence of humanity.

Though it might seem as though human life is too fragile to enter the premises, tours are conducted of Pripyat. To enter the area, visitors must first gain permission and get a pass. These are obtained by visiting a center one hundred kilometers away. Another issue coming to bare is the growing dilapidation of the buildings. Without regular care and maintenance, towers and apartment blocks are becoming less stable. Because workmen cannot enter the area without being contaminated, the buildings are increasingly at risk and visitors are presented with another threat should they wish to enter Pripyat.

As a tribute to the destructive power of mankind, the terror of Pripyat is perhaps more of a warning. Its existence – a ghost town that slowly inflicts cancer on those who stay too long – acts as a reminder of what might be should our global community collapse. While perhaps more of a Cold War concern, Pripyat is a thoroughly modern ghost town and one of the most dangerous and frankly terrifying places on the planet.

Hell Fire Club on Montpelier Hill, Ireland

From a very modern terror to a very traditional one, Ireland's Montpelier Hill is the home to many elements of the paranormal. Beyond the typical ghosts, however, perhaps the strangest thread of this rich historical cloth is the group known as the Hell Fire Club. This is the name given to a group who occupied the building built during the early 1700s, originally as a hunting lodge constructed by an Irish politician. The Hell Fire Club is a name that has been shared among many similar groups throughout the British Isles and Ireland, all of which have a history of witchcraft.

Today, all that is left behind seems to be a ruin. Whether this adds to the strangeness is in the eye of the beholder. It gives us a great idea of how the building once looked, however, with the upper floors hinting at the hall and reception rooms, while the eastern side had an extra story. The ground floor was left to the servants, while the building's main entrance is actually on the upper floor, made accessible by the long stretch of stairs. On the outside, there are stables and mounting blocks for the horses and the hunting parties. There was a courtyard for entertaining guests and workers. To the north, visitors can look over Dublin and Kildare, with the lodge sitting amid a one thousand-acre estate.

The history does not begin with the construction of the lodge, however. Archaeologists have uncovered traces of a prehistoric burial site on the top of the hill. The lodge is built right on top of this ancient grave. There was also a standing stone nearby, the kind of pagan artefact shared with locations such as Stonehenge. This was taken during the building process and used as a hearthstone in the making of the lodge's fireplace.

For those building the lodge, a warning might have been apparent as they approached completion. A great storm arrived and blew away the first roof they built. According to the local superstitions, this was held to be the devil's work. It was said that the devil demanded revenge against the men who had built a home on the site he held to be sacred. However, the builders were not deterred and soon replaced the former roof with an arched stone replacement. Even though most of the building has crumbled away, this roof still remains in place.

After completion, it is thought that the lodge was not actually used often. The owner – the man who had commissioned the project – passed away in 1729, and there are very few records of it being permanently inhabited during the time immediately after its completion. It was during this time, however, that the lodge's infamous association with the Hell Fire Club was born.

The Irish branch of the Hell Fire Club was founded in 1737 by a man named Richard Parsons, the first Earl of Rosse, who partnered with James Worsdale. It is thought that Lord Rosse took on the position of president of the Hell Fire Club, with Worsdale being his second in command. A portrait in the National Gallery of Ireland shows an early painting of the Club with five members sitting around a table. The Club's mascot was known to be a black cat, and though many of their initial meetings took place in the city of Dublin, it has been noted that there was always an empty chair left at every gathering, a seat left vacant for the devil himself.

Seeking out a new meeting place, the Hell Fire Club began to let the lodge from the family who had built it. The remote location of the lodge seems to have appealed to the Club, allowing them to hide many of their activities from the public eye. Because of this, very few records exist of their practices at the lodge. Again, we must turn to local folklore for an insight into what happened at the location. One of the most famous incidents involves a stranger lost in a storm. Coming across the lodge and seeking shelter, the Hell Fire Club invited the man into their lodge and asked him to take part in a game of cards. One of players dropped a card during the game. As he leaned down to retrieve the item, he noticed the stranger's foot was, in fact, a cloven hoof. Just as the player noticed the fact, the stranger vanished in a large puff of smoke and flame. He was never seen again.

A similar story involves a priest who journeyed to the home. When he gained entry into the building, he came across members of the club engaged in the ritual sacrifice of a black cat. Knowing this to be a satanic ritual, the priest snatched the cat from the crowd and began to utter an exorcism. As his words were unleashed, the body of the cat trembled and from the animal's mouth exited the shape of a demon, which vanished into the night. More stories of deals with the devil and such black magic have also involved Simon Luttrell, the Earl of Carhampton and Sheriff of Dublin. He is known to be the subject of the 1770s poem, The Diaboliad, which painted him as one of the worst men in England. If we are to believe local legend, Luttrell entered into a deal with the devil, sacrificing his soul for the settling of his debts. The final point at which the devil would reclaim his prize was the lodge. When Lucifer arrived, Luttrell played a trick, distracted the devil, and ran away. In addition to these stories, more grounded accounts of drunken lechery and black masses involving the sacrifice of animals and even – on one occasion – the sacrifice of a dwarf have all been attributed to Montpelier Hill.

After the growing reputation the Hell Fire Club brought to the lodge, we know that the building was damaged by a serious fire. Explaining the incident is difficult, with different stories being given as to the reason for the fire. One such story involves the Club themselves setting the building to flame when their reputation resulted in their lease not being renewed. Another suggests the Club wanted to give the lodge a "hellish" aesthetic quality to ward off visitors. The third version puts forth the idea that a servant spilled a drink on a member during a black mass. In retaliation, the member poured brandy over the servant and burned him alive. Struggling, the burning man ran through the home and set numerous places alight. The blaze supposedly killed many people, but the Hell Fire Club themselves denied any involvement with any such stories.

After a brief hiatus, the Hell Fire Club returned to their activities in 1771, often changing their name to the Holy Fathers and back again. Montpelier Hill remained the meeting place of choice among the group, with the next series of legends involving murders, kidnaps and even cannibalism, though we only have scant details passed down among locals. Whatever the truth of the matter, the Club and the lodge were becoming notorious. Stories of satanic rituals and black magic – whether true or not – were inextricably linked to Montpelier Hill.

However, over the years, the lodge fell into a bad way. The building needed a great deal of attention. The reputation of the lodge was enough to garner interest, and even during the 1700s, Montpelier Hill was famed enough that those fascinated by the dark arts would visit the empty building to test themselves by spending a night in the lodge. Ever since, it has passed through various hands, inherited and sold as the fortunes of the local landowners rise and fall. The one thing that has remained is the reputation the Hell Fire Club brought to the building. Because of this interest, the current owner has installed hand rails and warning signs in the ruined lodge to ward off interested parties. Some people still try themselves, testing whether they can manage a night in the ruins, surrounded by a history of murder and devil worship. Of all the places in Ireland, few possess the satanic history of the Hell Fire Club's lodge on top of Montpelier Hill.

The Ridges, USA

When discussing the most unexplainable and horrible places in the world, insane asylums hold a certain high rank in the list. Even more deserving of inclusion is the idea of an abandoned insane asylum. With previous generations not possessing today's better understanding of treatment when it comes to mental health conditions, the practices of our forebears when dealing with the insane were more than questionable. With murders, ill treatment, and the prevalence of the criminally mad in these places, the idea of visiting an abandoned asylum is very low on many people's wish lists.

The first of these places we will examine is the Athens Lunatic Asylum in Ohio, commonly referred to as the

Ridges. Open from 1874 until it closed in 1993, the building has a history of housing patients who simply did not fit in with conventional society. During the time it was open, the asylum provided a form of care to everyone from soldiers scarred by the Civil War to criminals who were deemed too insane to be allowed in a typical prison. Today, despite their terrifying past, many of the buildings are used for administrative purposes for the local museums and universities. But it is the history of the building that provides the real scare.

The Athens Lunatic Asylum has a particular reputation as being the home of one of medicine's darkest and most condemned practices – the lobotomy. In addition to the practice of removing small pieces of patient's brains, the Ridges have also housed a number of paranormal sightings.

Let's look at the early years of the hospital first. Opening in January of 1874, the buildings first appeared under the name "The Athens Hospital for the Insane." It would pass through a variety of different titles during its time, with the name "The Ridges" seemingly deriving from a competition held in the local community to put a familiar and less intimidating name to the increasingly scary building. Growing from an early plot of just over one hundred and forty acres, the hospital would eventually span over a thousand. The need for a hospital for the insane emerged soon after the end of the Civil War. In an effort to become a self-sustaining facility, there have been various attempts over the past hundred years to introduce farming, livestock, orchards, dairies, greenhouses, and similar food production means to the grounds. Originally, the buildings were split into three departments. A wing for the men, a wing for the women, and a collection of smaller buildings to house the administration staff. Over time, the ability to house many patients grew and grew, leading it to become one of the biggest mental health facilities in the state. One of the factors that leads to the building's intimidating façade today is the influence of Victorian architecture and planning into the original designs, which present a stark and austere approach to a facility seemingly designed primarily for care. This should give an insight into the level of tenderness applied to many of the facility's patients over time.

Those who have poured over the information left behind by the various staff members throughout the years have gained an insight into the kind of practices used to treat mental health problems during the last century. There is a notable shift in the 1950s towards medication as a means of treatment rather than physiological methods, but this meant many of the patients were drugged and subdued and thus unable to run the farms and greenhouses needed to keep the facility self-sustaining. There is also a key insight into the abilities of the staff. We know from the documents that, while some were fully trained and accredited, other staff members had no training at all. Certain members of the staff lived on-site, while others commuted to work each day.

Possibly the most important insight from these historical documents, however, goes some way to confirming many people's worst fears about the ways patients were treated during the past. Methods such as electroshock, lobotomy, hydrotherapy, and psychotropic drugs were all used to address patients' symptoms. Most of these methods have been discredited by the modern medical community.

For patients committed during the 1800s, one of the main causes of insanity is listed as masturbation, followed by intemperance and dissipation. To reflect these loose definitions of insanity, the first three years of the hospital saw eighty-one male patients committed, as well as one woman, all of whom had their insanity diagnosed as being due to masturbation in some regard. For women, the third most popular diagnosis was listed as menstrual derangements, which saw twenty-nine women declared insane.

Due to the scarce understanding of the troubles of mental health during much of the buildings opening, many of the diagnoses were inaccurate and many of the treatments unsuitable. It was not uncommon for families to simply drop off elderly relatives when they could no longer afford to care for them or for parents to commit rebellious teens who defied their familial instructions. This willingness to declare people insane led to the building being three times more crowded than it had been intended. Overflowing with patients, many of whom had been rendered less than functional by lobotomies, the standard of patient care dropped.

As with any aging building that has hosted what many have described as medically sanctioned torture, the tales of ghosts and hauntings have grown within the local community. Thanks to the building's condemned appearance, as well as its history of questionable treatment, many people in the area have long described how patients and staff alike are still lining the hallways, long after they have departed. Even though the location is now used by various bodies for differing projects, the Ridges still maintain their reputation as a destination for the insane and as a home of some of the country's most shameful and most insane methods of treating some of society's most at-risk members.

If ever you venture into the Ridges after dark, the howls and the screams of those being lobotomized apparently still echo around the halls. Or maybe they might be the sounds of an escaped patient, returning to the building that caused them so much harm. With such a long and checkered past, any trip to the Ridges is beset by the knowledge of the horrific practices and treatments used by those who were trusted the most.

Byberry Mental Asylum, USA

Another entry in our list, the Philadelphia State Hospital at Byberry shares many terrifying attributes with the Ridges. With a history ranging from the earliest parts of the twentieth century, the treatments and practices used by many of the doctors were very similar, with the now abandoned building sharing many of the same ghost stories that haunt the Ohio facility. Holding as many as seven thousand patients during its most popular moments, the potential for scary histories and lingering hauntings is not to be overlooked.

The key difference, perhaps, in the case of this building when compared to other asylums is that we know the extent to which patients were mistreated at Byberry. Of the several investigations that have examined conditions in the hospital, it has been discovered that not only did raw sewage line the building's hallways, but also the patients were forced to sleep in these halls, while the staff continuously mistreated and exploited those placed under their care. Actions such as these have led to the building being featured in many accounts of America's most haunted buildings.

Beginning life as a building designed to help those suffering from mental health problems, the initial farmstead was soon turned into a full asylum. The first building work began in 1906, with physician Dr. Benjamin Rush being placed in control of the facility. It was his belief that, like conventional diseases, mental health issues could be treated. However, patients would need to be kept away from outsiders until Rush considered them healed.

In the 1930s, the institution was placed under government control. At this point, it was noted that conditions in the asylum were not good. There had been allegations made that patients had been abused and that the manner of treatment was inhumane. During the 1940s, this became a national issue, with a man named Charlie Lord, an orderly, managing to take several undercover photographs of the conditions the patients lived in. This collection of thirty-six photographs featured many images that disturbed the public. Dozens of naked men were herded together into groups. It became clear that excrement was lining many of the hallways. The photos came to the attention of the First Lady Eleanor Roosevelt, who pledged to address the issues. The photos were later printed in an issue of Life magazine, provoking outrage from the public. Author Albert Deutsch recalled witnessing the conditions and likened them to images taken at the Nazi concentration camps. He mentioned in particular the herding of the patients and the fetid, awful stench.

From this point on, the institution was doomed. It would begin a gradual downsizing process set to take place across a number of decades. It did, however, manage to continue into the 1980s, when reports of abuse and maltreatment were still rampant. A patient recalled having a tooth pulled without being given any form of anesthetic. More investigations and inspections were carried out, with many officials and workers being fired and dismissed.

It was announced that Byberry Asylum would be closed in a press conference on December 7, 1987. In their statement, officials described the conditions inside the asylum as being "atrocious" and "irreversible." With closure seemingly imminent, the actual process was held up by what has been described as "patient issues," the most pressing of which was the fact that two patients had been discovered dead just two days after being released. The remaining patients were transferred to nearby facilities, and the doors were finally shut.

Despite this closure, the buildings were not demolished. The site of many decades of abuse and atrocious conditions, the asylum still stood in the same place, though it was condemned and people were forbidden from entering. Demolition was held up by concerns over the asbestos used during construction. As such, looters were able to enter and made a point of stealing anything of value (such as copper piping). Once there was nothing of value left, those who entered the building amused themselves by smashing, crashing, and setting fires.

By the turn of the century, the abandoned asylum had earned a reputation as one of the country's scariest locations. The now smashed and burned wards still bore the scars of the various treatments throughout the years. Reports of ghosts haunting the corridors were common, and people went out of their way to visit the facility. There were even tips found on the internet for those visiting, making suggestions about how to best gain entry to the building. By 2003, every pane of glass in every window had fallen victim to the vandals. Anything flammable, like mattresses or chairs, had been burned. Graffiti lined every wall where the patients had once left their trails of excrement. While boards were placed over the windows to prevent anyone else entering, they just made it hard to detect those who were already inside.

In 2006, the decision was taken to demolish the Byberry Asylum. The contractors not only had to knock down the walls, but also had to remove the tons of asbestos and lead paint that had been used to form the walls. In a building dedicated to treating the ill, the health hazards were built into the very walls of the institution.

These days, there are very few traces of the asylum left on the site. That is not to say that the location has become any more welcoming, however. If you are to believe the locals, the ill-feeling and the dead who previously haunted the Byberry asylum have taken instead to wandering the grounds. Now surrounded by stark, dead trees and demolished buildings, the once-horrific asylum has left its scars on the landscape and the local psyche as much as anything else. If you are searching for one of the darkest moments in America's past and the effect it still has to this day, then a visit to Byberry might be essential.

The Beechworth Lunatic Asylum, Australia

Lunatic Asylum Beechworth

Our final entry into this trio of terrifying asylums is located outside of America. For this entry, we turn to the town of Beechworth in Australia, several hours outside of Melbourne. The Beechworth Lunatic Asylum is thought to be one of the most haunted locations in Australia, with ghosts of patients and staff frightening visitors for many years.

Also known as the Mayday Hills Hospital, this is the second oldest of all of the asylums in the state of Victoria. Its history dates back to the year of 1867, when it first opened and stretched half a kilometer from end to end. Designed to hold twelve hundred patients when at capacity (half of each gender), it has been reported that as many as three thousand people died within the walls during the one hundred and twenty-eight years that it treated the mentally ill. But what can visitors expect when they journey to the place that is now a simple admin building?

One of the most famous treasures found in the walls is the signature of famed outlaw, J. Kelly, the uncle of Ned. His name is cut into a pane of glass after he had been committed to the asylum for burning down the house of his sister-in-law. A young Ned Kelly was in the home at the time. For the crime, he was sentenced to fifteen years of hard labor, much of which was spent building the hospital itself. By the time his work was finished, the criminal was in such a fragile mental condition that he spent the rest of his days as a patient at the facility.

One of the residents who would later be said to haunt the walls is the specter of Matron Sharpe. Reported as having been seen in numerous places around the grounds, the Matron was said to have been one of the kinder caregivers at the hospital, a notable difference from many who worked alongside her. Perhaps it is this concern for her patients that compelled her to stay in Beechworth and watch over her wards.

A patient who has also been spied around the grounds is Tommy Kennedy, a well-liked and friendly inmate who was eventually allowed the job of working in the kitchens. This would be where he would die, an unfortunate accident killing Tommy before his time. To this day, it is suggested, Tommy Kennedy haunts the grounds and tugs at the clothes and ribs of children in the area.

Around the grounds, it was the Reaction Hall that was one of the patients' favorite areas. A place designed for their entertainment, this was a room for singing, music, theatre and – on Sundays – became a small chapel. It was turned into a cinema in 1939 for patients to watch films, and to this day, it is the famed location of two of the asylum's most notorious ghosts. One is only seen by those on the inside, when the specter of a small girl approaches a window and taps gently on the glass. The other ghost is seen when looking into the hall from outside, an elderly gentleman who turns his back on anyone who looks directly in through the windows. It has not been possible to determine the identities of these people.

While patients might have loved the Reaction Hill, the Grevillia Wing has the opposite effect. Now forbidden for visitors' entry, it had been condemned for thirteen years. When functioning, it was the room the patients feared most. With a lack of medication during the institution's early years, this was where doctors and nurses used electroshock treatment on those deemed mentally ill. This process involved direction bolts of electricity concentrated through a patient's temples in an effort to "correct" their thought patterns. It has since been proven to have nothing but detrimental effects, but at certain points, the entire patient population of the asylum received this treatment. Shocks could be so powerful as to break bones and shatter teeth. In this wing, there are two more commonly seen ghosts.

The first is the spirit of a doctor who wanders through the corridors of the Grevillia wing on some nights. The second is the aforementioned Matron Sharpe, who was typically seen by fellow nurses when the hospital was still open. It has been suggested that her presence in the ice cold electroshock room is a soothing and warm presence. It seems that, even in death, the patients and their ghosts know to steer clear of their hated wing.

One specter who can be traced stems from the death of a patient. The woman was a committed smoker and was thrown to her death by another patient who had demanded the woman's cigarettes for himself. The deceased woman was Jewish, and as such, doctors were not allowed to move the body until a Rabbi was present. This meant that the patient's corpse was left outside the building for two days while the Rabbi arrived from nearby Melbourne. The ghost of the woman has been spotted by several witnesses and is said to haunt the spot where her body hit the floor.

The final tale of a ghost in the grounds of Beechwood is perhaps the most grizzly of all. A patient disappeared from the hospital, prompting a large-scale search, but it came to no avail. Many weeks later, however, the asylum's resident dog was found tugging on the decomposed leg of a corpse near the gated entrance to the institution. A further search found that the leg had fallen from the rest of the body, which was in a tree above the leg. The corpse was decomposing at such a rate that the leg had simply dropped off. These days, that same man seems to stroll the same area of the grounds, making himself known to visitors.

Of all the asylums we have examined in this book, many are worrying, disturbing, and eerie places. It is Beechwood, however, that seems to be the most "classically" haunted. Home to a number of ghosts that have been sighted by many people, the insane asylums of the past have provided fertile searches for the most terrifying location on the planet.

Lome Bazaar, Togo

And now, we'll make a visit to Africa. While many Western locations in this book focus on ghost stories and western mythologies, folklores and magic, the similar spiritualties we find in Africa can be equally as terrifying. While many of the Western locations are notable for their atmosphere during the darkest nights, the Lome Bazaar in Togo is just as terrifying in the blazing heat of the West African sun.

As the epicenter of one of the world's most misunderstood magical arts, the bazaar in Lome is the place for people to pick and choose all of the ingredients they might need for the practice of voodoo. Not just a branch of witchcraft, voodoo is also a commonly practiced religion in the area. The paraphernalia needed to adhere to the religion can be bought from this market place. For the uninitiated, however, the stacks of animal skulls can be a horrifying encounter.

The remains of animals provide a spiritual quality to those who do their shopping in this section of Lome. They can be used to protect the wielder from diseases and all manner of evil. By congregating in the market, voodoo practitioners can function much like any other supermarket, picking and choosing what they need in one location. Among the various remains, those of the crocodiles, monkeys, owls, snakes, vultures, and cats are used for various purposes.

It might be of some relief to people that the animals themselves are not actually killed on location. Instead, they are collected from the surrounding areas and brought to the bazaar location to sell to as many people as possible.

Key to the practice of voodoo are the elements of earth, air, fire, and water, with the traditional healers able to use the ingredients to fashion medicines, talismans, and other artefacts using the remains. While they might appear horrifying to the uninitiated, their importance to local magical practices makes them common place to many who frequent the market.

One of the key results of the voodoo arts is the black powder. This is created by grinding down the various animal heads, mixing them with herbs, and then setting them on fire. To achieve the best results, the heads of various animals including vultures and owls are used, in addition to cobras and vipers. To treat people, voodoo practitioners cut the ill person's back or chest three times. Once the wound is open, the black powder is rubbed into the wound and the flesh.

Another common ailment demands help with various fertility issues. For those who might be struggling to conceive a child, turning to a hospital might not provide the desired results. Instead, people turn to their local voodoo market, where something is conjured using the wares on display in Lome.

There are even charms used during sports. For soccer goalkeepers, a chimpanzee's hand can be used to bring good luck. Locals use the left hand of the chimp (or in some cases, a gorilla), prepare it with certain herbs, and then secrete it about the body of the goalkeeper. It is designed to improve the speed of his reactions. Similar spells are used for long distance runners, using the head, legs, and heart of a horse.

One common sight in Lome market is bones. They come in every shape and size, from the smallest snake backbone to the legs of elephants. There are even rumors that people may be able to sell the bones of a human with the right contacts and the right cash. The largest bones are a protective device. They are used in homes, often in the form of small statues, to deliver a protective aura on any household in which they reside.

Even to the well-acquainted, the voodoo bazaar of Lome is one of the strangest and most horrific locations on earth. Rather than something secret and sinister, it is a market of death, designed to propagate the use of magic using the scariest of ingredients.

Oradour-sur-Glane, France

The haunting locations we have looked at so far are often ruins that have fallen into disrepair or buildings whose reputations means no one will go near it. However, in the case of Oradour-sur-Glane, the stark buildings have been left standing and visitors have been encouraged so that future generations will learn of just how capable of evil and destruction man can be.

We begin the story in the late stages of the Second World War. It was 1944 when the Second SS Panzer Division of the German Army was stationed in the town of Valence-d'Agen in the south of France. Of the divisions units, it is the fourth Grenadier Regiment named after the Führer himself that takes the key role in the story. While waiting to be resupplied, the commanding officers were informed of the rumor that a captured German officer was being held in the nearby town of Oradour-sur-Glane. The Germans gathered together thirty French citizens whom they could use to exchange for the captured solider and set off towards the nearby town. But this was just a ruse to justify what would be coming.

The fateful day was June 10. The German battalion formed a seal around Oradour-sur-Glane and made it known to the people that they were required to assemble in the center of the town. Here, they would have their papers examined. As well as the residents, six cyclists who happened to be passing through the town were collected and taken to the gathering point in the town square. Once everyone was in place, the women and the children were separated and placed inside the church. The doors were locked. German soldiers began the process of looting the town, while the French men were taken to a collection of nearby barns. Machine guns had been set up here and the citizens were gunned down. It has even been reported by one survivor that the Germans were instructed to shoot for the legs, so as to prolong the death of the townsmen. Once the citizens were suitably immobile, they were covered in fuel and set alight. While six people were said to have escaped (one of whom was shot hours later) it is reported that one hundred and ninety people were massacred inside those barns.

Not finished, the Germans returned to the church which housed the women and the children. They placed an incendiary device on the building. When the Germans' plan became apparent, some tried to escape through windows and doors but were gunned down by the surrounding soldiers. In addition to the men, two hundred and forty-seven women were killed and two hundred and five children perished with them. One woman, Marguerite Rouffanche, got away with her life. She escaped by crawling to a pea bush behind the church, severely injured. Here, she hid through the night and awaited the rescue forces that would arrive the next day. While they departed, the Germans attempted to raze the town. Rescue forces arrived too late and over six hundred people had died.

It would be a few days before the survivors would be able to gather together to bury the dead. Some had been lucky enough to flee at the first sight of the approaching army, though six hundred and forty two townsfolk had perished. It had only taken a few hours.

Of the information we have today regarding the event, one of the most important is the report of Raymond Murphy, an American airman whose plane was shot down over France around this time. He had been found by the French Resistance and when it was finally possible, he was moved to England. Here, he gave an account of what he had seen in a formal report. The final version included handwritten addendum, in which Murphy recounted witnessing the site of a brutal murder of French citizens. As well as the five hundred men, women, and children he described as murdered by the Germans, he mentions spotting a baby who had been crucified. Murphy's is the only account to mention the crucifixion and was only made public in 2011. Despite not naming the town, authorities are sure that the site he is referring to is Oradour-sur-Glane, as well as being confident in the veracity of his statement.

Back in the 1940s, the German response to the incident reflects a similar level of disgust to the reaction of the Allies. Erwin Rommel was just one high-ranking Nazi who made his displeasure at the army's actions known. An investigation into the actions of the company was launched. This investigation was cancelled within a few days when most of the men involved perished during a battle.

After the cessation of the war, a military tribunal was held in Bordeaux to discuss the testimonies of the sixty-five soldiers who remained alive from the German forces who had attacked Oradour-sur-Glane that day. The date for the trial was January 12 1953. Only twenty one of the sixty-five men were present at the hearing, due to the fact that many were living in the untouchable, Soviet-controlled Eat Germany at the time. Extradition was banned, so the hearing was held in their absence. It is interesting to note that – of those present – only seven were fully fledged Germans. Fourteen were Alsatians, Frenchmen of German descent who had been incorporated into the German army. All but one of these Alsatians claimed they had been forced to join the Nazis.

The trial itself was the focus of a huge amount of attention in Alsace, with this attention demanding that the French authorities hold two separate trials. One would be held for the Alsatians and one for the Germans. Despite twenty of those on trial being found guilty, fellow Alsatians protested what they saw as their fellow countrymen being "press ganged" into a foreign army and being forced to carry out the actions. As such, the French commuted the sentences of the men from Alsace.

Most importantly of all, however, is the decision regarding what would be done with the town. A literal ruin with no citizens left to inhabit the burned out homes, it was decided that the buildings would remain in place. Not only would they be a memorial to those who had died in one of the war's many, many crimes against humanity, but it would serve as a reminder of the dark acts of which humanity is capable. Future generations would be able to look upon the town and see the full extent of the brutality of the Nazis and the occupation.

While it might seem strange to include it on a list alongside ghost towns and haunted asylums, there are few entries on the list which have seen crimes as severe as those committed in Oradour-sur-Glane. People who visit the area mention the quiet chills that come over the body when walking through the barns or the church where so many people were killed before their time. The whole town itself is now a tribute to the terror that man is capable of inflicting on his fellow man.

The Bhangarh Fort, India

The idea of a haunted building is not uncommon, with many castles and forts across Europe possessing a multitude of ghosts. It should come as no surprise in buildings that have both housed many people and been the locations of so many battles, that those who died on the site would linger on in some respect. But one of the more interesting and horrifying examples comes from India.

While it might be three hundred kilometers from Delhi, the fort in Bhangarh is considered close to the capital in such a large country. Nowadays, the fort is not visited by many people, with the remote location and lack of any real tourism only adding to the eeriness and the strangeness built into the walls. To reach the destination, travelers must use their own mapping skills and advice from the locals.

For those who are considering making the trip, the passage past Gurgaon is relatively easy, with few people encountering any problems until they reach the Alwar district in Rajasthan. If anything, the long journey provides visitors ample opportunity to think over all of the possibilities that await them at their destination.

One factor that does affect many people who make the trip is the weather. Ranging from sweltering heat to huge storms, the first looks at the fort can come under the anvil of the sun or the pounding of the rain. To add to the problems, certain sections of the road are not tarmacked and lead to bumpy, rough journeys.

With such heavy rains, visibility can often shrink to just five hundred meters. While this might sound like enough to move, it hinders travel when there is little in the way of road signs pointing you towards your destination. All of this leads to a greater sense of dread as you approach the fort, with the weather itself almost willing away visitors and preventing them entering into the building.

Next to the entrance to the main gate is a Hindu temple. All across the grounds are at least six temples, all set up to raise awareness for different facets of the faith. The one at the gate is dedicated to Hanuman, while others are set up for Gopinath, Someswar, and other figures in the Hindu faith. For the locals, the temples do nothing to dissuade the reputation of the building, which has come to be known as the fort of ghosts.

In the immediate entrance are spacers for dancers and market stalls. They are a reminder that at one time, this was a fully functioning community, though the members are now long dead. The fort was first built (or at least, this incarnation) during the late 1500s. With such a long and storied history, the amount of local folklore surrounding the fort is incredible. There are even suggestions that the local community vanished one day, obliterated in one fell swoop. With no records to indicate what actually happened to the original community, it is one theory among many.

Today, there are a few families who live on the grounds of the fort. They make a living entertaining those few tourists who do arrive in the area, and they share their homes occasionally with the local animals who wander into the fort. For them, the biggest issue is that the building does not have access to electricity, a hindrance but also a hint to the ancient history incumbent in the walls.

Technically, all night time visitors are banned, with a sign being fixed at the front of the gate from the Archaeological Survey of India telling people that visiting the building is not allowed after dark or before sunset. This is backed up by the locals, who say that no visitors who have stayed within the walls have made it through the night.

But what of the real hauntings? Local legend suggests that the fort was once the victim of a wizard who practiced black magic. He cursed the people living in the fort and told them all that they would meet an unnatural death, with their souls doomed to haunt the building for the rest of time. With the community seemingly having vanished at some point in the past, we know little about the actual events that took place in this building. What we do know is that those who are left behind are either few in number or reticent to spend too much time in the building. As one of India's most haunted locations, it remains a popular destination for those who can get there. While it might seem accommodating during the day, there is a reason why so few people are willing to spend the night within the walls.

Unit 731, China

The inclusions in this collection have tried to present those unknown locations around the world where the paranormal, the horrific, and the chilling all come together. While certain entries lean towards the paranormal, others lean towards the horrific. Of all those included, perhaps none is quite as chilling or as innocuously named as Unit 731 in China. In the West, we all know about the horrible acts committed during World War II. We have looked at one of them already. But we often forget about the Pacific Theatre of the War, especially the events that took place on mainland China. If you have never read about Unit 731 before, it might be advisable to reconsider whether you really want to read beyond this point.

Described as a covert laboratory dedicated to the study of chemical and biological warfare, Unit 731 was essentially a research and development department whose aim was to determine the limits of the human body. Established and used during the Second Sin-Japanese War (part of the Second World War), the unit was controlled by the Imperial Japanese Army. Here, many of Japan's most notorious war crimes were committed.

The site chosen for Unit 731 was near Harbin, the biggest city in the country of Manchukuo (the puppet state set up during the Japanese invasion of China.) During the time the unit was operational, thousands of people passed through the doors. We do not know exactly how many people – men, women and children – were killed, but it is said to have numbered anywhere from three to twelve thousand. This was just one of the medical experimentation sites used by the Japanese, but it is perhaps the worst.

The story of Unit 731 begins with the vision of a single individual. Shiro Ishii was thought to be an extremely intelligent young person all throughout his academic career. Standing at six feet tall, he was taller than many of his Japanese counterparts, considered a veritable giant. His studies took him to Kyoto Imperial University, where he focused on pathology, bacteriology, serology, and preventative medicine. An early example of his work involved a trip to Kyushu, where a disease was ravaging the local community. Prevented from examining his patients in great detail – the brain would swell and deter his diagnoses – he instead turned his attention to the water supply and introduced a filtration system designed to eliminate parasites. This was hugely successful, and Ishii was noted as a rising star. He was asked to demonstrate his invention before the Emperor himself, a great honor. One of his tricks was to urinate into his filter and then drink the results, so confident was he in the technology he had developed. Following this success, he left Japan in 1928 to travel the world. He spent two years visiting clinics in thirty countries across the globe. This information he would take back to Japan.

Ishii possessed firm relationships with many prominent government officials in the military, including Nobuyoshi Araki, the future War Minister. This allowed him to secure funding for many of his research projects which, he said, were intended to help the prosperity of his country. His work, he hoped, would turn Japan into a dominant global force. One of the main focuses of his collaborations and his research projects would be biological and chemical warfare, discovering ways of using his scientific knowledge to further Japan's military ambitions.

He would soon have a proving ground for his research. The Japanese invasion of Manchuria occurred in 1931 and led to the establishment of Manchukuo on mainland China. Outside of Japan, this location would provide Ishii with all of the resources he would need to further his research. In a secret location, Unit 731 was to be set up as a testing ground for Ishii's new approaches to chemical and biological warfare. The first iteration of the unit was destroyed by rebellious prisoners who blew up part of the lab. The second unit was designed with extra security in mind. To the public, it was known as "Epidemic Prevention and Water Supply Unit of the Kwantung Army," a deceptive and misleading title. Ishii was placed in charge of the unit. Around him, the war was beginning to escalate.

Unit 731 was founded across three square kilometers, all hidden behind a large perimeter wall. In addition to this, high voltage electric fences lined the property. People were not allowed in or out without express permission. In all, there were close to a hundred and fifty structures, including prisoner housing, animal houses, an air strip, and an incinerator. Secrecy was an essential part of the unit. Workers were moved in and out of the facility in covered cargo trucks from which the registration plates and identification markers were removed or frequently changed.

One research project involved Ishii searching the best method of dispersing a virus. He came to the summation that using a local water supply to disperse internal pathogens was best (more effective than air-based solutions). Such experiments would prove to be useful in the war. As well as a research facility, it became a production hotbed. At certain points, it was creating close to three hundred kilos of bacteria and germs designed to be harmful. When in full flow, the facility could produce more than enough chemical weapons to destroy all life on Earth several times. When researching plagues, Ishii discovered the benefits of contaminating fleas, who could disseminate his diseases quicker than he might have ever imagined. To reach his conclusions, he began not only testing on fleas, but testing on the captured Chinese prisoners who had been placed into his care.

The use of Chinese prisoners in Ishii's experiments was hidden from the majority of employees. Tunnels and secret passages were used to move the doomed prisoners around the camp, the final destinations being blocks seven and eight, where the experiments took place. As well as captured Chinese prisoners, Russians who were unable to give up valuable information were transferred to Ishii from local detention camps. He even began to trick locals into bringing themselves to the unit. With offers of employment, he would encourage men, women, children, the elderly, and even pregnant women to arrive at the facility. They would never leave.

From what witness accounts we have of the condition of the prisoners, we know that they were not treated well. There are reports of rotting limbs, of bones poking out through dead skin, of high fevers and sweating, of people writhing around the floor in agony and pain.

People who had been exposed to respiratory infections coughed constantly. Various other victims were emaciated and skeletal or bloated and starving. Many had open wounds and blisters. Cells were communal, so prisoners were thrown together, infectious or not. This would allow Ishii and his scientist to monitor how quickly diseases spread. Some prisoners tried to institute invented medical care, but they were prevented. For female prisoners, rape was a daily occurrence, with the guards sexually abusing them on a regular basis. All the while, doctors spread various diseases via food, water, air, insects, or many other methods conjured up at Unit 731.

A visiting scientist named Dr. Sueo Akimoto described the way in which doctors at Unit 731 functioned. In recalling what he saw at the facility, he remembers being "shocked" at seeing the extent of the human experiments. He mentions the lack of conscience of the medical staff who treated the patients/victims/prisoners like animals. They were, he suggests, essentially sentenced to death. For the doctors, these deaths were deemed honorable, as they contributed to the furthering of medical knowledge. Akimoto tried to resign several times, but this was refused by his superiors. Despite his experiments not involving humans, he still sought to get out as soon as possible.

Thanks to accounts such as that of Dr. Sueo Akimoto, we do have an understanding of the various human experimentation that did take place at Unit 731. Of the worst atrocities committed at the facility, these include:

- Vivisection without anesthesia – the dissecting of live patients to learn more about the way the body functions. These dissections were performed while the prisoners were alive as it was believed that the decomposition process might affect results. Men, women, children, and infants were subject to this kind of vivisection.

- Dissections and experiments were performed on pregnant women, who had often been impregnated by the guards and the doctors themselves.
- Prisoners' limbs were amputated to further the way the body reacts to losing blood.

- The limbs that were detached from one prisoner were often reattached to another, to study whether it would be possible to transfer body parts.

- Frequently, prisoners would have their body parts frozen solid using chemicals and processes. They were then amputated and thawed, with doctors noting the effect of gangrene and decomposition.

- Some victims would have their stomachs removed from their bodies while still alive.

- Some prisoners were hung in an upside down position to find out how long it would be before they choked to death.
- Horse urine was directly injected into the kidneys of some prisoners.

- Starvation and its effects were frequently studied, simply by leaving prisoners without any form of food in their cells.

- Temperatures were a focus of many investigations, both high and low. Frost bite was an interest of the doctors, as well as the effect of temperature on the decay rates of the human body. Prisoners were often tested to see how well they could survive in extreme conditions.

- High levels of radiation and x-rays were given to patients in order to determine the points at which this exposure would be lethal.

In addition to these myriad human experiments, it is thought that close to four thousand further Chinese civilians were killed due to exposure to viruses and diseases developed at Ishii's Unit 731. These infections included anthrax and cholera, spread using everything from infected paper to tainted water. As well as this, there are hundreds of stories of the depravity of Ishii's experiments and those of his staff.

When Soviet Russia invaded Manchukuo at the close of the Second World War, Ishii and his staff began to destroy evidence. They fled to Japan with suicide capsules and the instruction that they must take their secrets to the grave. The Japanese even tried to demolish the unit with explosions as they exited, but the buildings were well constructed enough that they largely survived. At the close of the war, the scientists of Unit 731 were caught between the Soviets and the Americans. They struck a deal with the American authorities. In exchange for immunity and being kept from the Russians, they would share the knowledge of chemical warfare they had gained. The Americans pressed no charges for the crimes committed at Unit 731. The Soviets, however, held trials of their own with those they had captured. Scientists were sentenced to hard labor in Siberia for the crimes they had committed.

In the coming years, the public began to learn the truth about what Ishii and his team had done to their prisoners at Unit 731.

The buildings themselves were eventually bulldozed. In their place, a collection of uninteresting and unassuming buildings were constructed. Despite this, the area still bares traces of the experiments of Ishii and the rest of the team of scientists. Unlike the museum as Auschwitz, the crimes committed at Unit 731 are not as widely remembered. For those interested in the most chilling and traumatic places across the world, the location of one of humanities darkest pursuits of scientific knowledge ranks higher than most.

Conclusion

As we have seen throughout this book, the strangest, most horrible, and scariest places on the planet do not form one distinct pattern. As well as the paranormal, the reality of humanity can be just as chilling. For those who wish to visit these sites, being of a strong constitution is essential.

If you have a further interest in some of the world's scariest places, the reading list attached below is a fine indicator of what else lurks in the far flung corners of the planet. If you find yourself truly interested, the best solution is often to visit for yourself. Whether you wish to subject yourself to the witchcraft of Montpelier Hill, the bone piles of Lome Bazaar, or the scarred history of Unit 731, the world is certainly a scarier place than you might ever have imagined.

References

Adams, P. and Brazil, E. (2013). Extreme hauntings. Stroud: History Press.

Bartlett, S. (n.d.). Supernatural.

Belanger, J. (2011). The world's most haunted places. Pompton Plains, NJ: New Page Books.

Davis, J. and Queen, S. (n.d.). Haunted asylums, prisons, and sanatoriums.

Dunne, J. and Marsden, S. (2001). A ghost watcher's guide to Ireland. Gretna, La.: Pelican Pub. Co.

Gilabert, R. (2008). Oradour-sur-Glane. Albi: Un Autre reg'art.

Gold, H. (1996).Unit 731 testimony. Boston: Tuttle.

Hebras, R. (2001). Oradour-sur-Glane. Saintes: les Chemins de la memoire ed.

Lord, B. (2010).Hill of Crosses in Lithuania (Miracles of the Cross). Journeys of Faith.

Mittica, P., Rosenblum, N., Bertell, R. and Tchertkoff, W. (2007). Chernobyl. [London, Eng.]: Trolley.

Osorio-Robin, S., Gely, J. and Vire, M. (2014). Au coeur des tenebres. Paris: Paris musees.

Polidori, R. and Culbert, E. (2003). Zones of exclusion. Gottingen: Steidl.

Rees, L. (2001). Horror in the East. London: BBC.

Thomas, G., Langlume, D. and Gaffard, E. (2011).The catacombs of Paris. Paris: Parigramme.

Vernor, E. (n.d.). Haunted asylums.

Williams, P. and Wallace, D. (1989). Unit 731. London: Hodder & Stoughton.

Photography credits

Island of the Dolls, Mexico

http://img.weburbanist.com/wp-
content/uploads/2010/10/island-of-the-dolls-7.jpg
http://i.ytimg.com/vi/C0jHbf6MQeI/maxresdefault.jpg

Hill of Crosses, Ukraine

http://upload.wikimedia.org/wikipedia/commons/7/7b/Sia
uliai_Hill_of_Crosses.JPG

Ahokigahara, Japan

http://upload.wikimedia.org/wikipedia/commons/thumb/b/
bf/Aokigahara_forest_01.jpg/1280px-
Aokigahara_forest_01.jpg

Hell Fire Club Montpelier Hill, Ireland

http://upload.wikimedia.org/wikipedia/commons/b/b1/Hell
_Fire_Club_Dublin_at_Dawn.jpg
http://upload.wikimedia.org/wikipedia/commons/c/c2/Mo
ntpelier-Hill-after-sunset.jpg

The Ridges, USA

http://6932024ba42556b26407-a85c761a6bd49913b8d52eb0d7ddeadd.r85.cf2.rackcdn.com/E25D59ED-750D-48C3-BBE5-578D8E8B2CC7.jpg

https://www.flickr.com/photos/7687126@N06/3195467574

Byberry Asylum

http://www.asylumprojects.org/images/d/df/byberrybbuildingviolentwarddayroom.jpg

http://www.philadelphiastatehospital.com/sitebuildercontent/sitebuilderpictures/E389.JPG

Beechworth Lunatic Asylum

http://upload.wikimedia.org/wikipedia/commons/6/68/Beechworthasylum.jpg

http://upload.wikimedia.org/wikipedia/commons/f/f0/Yarrabendhaha.jpg

Lomo Bazaar, Togo

http://upload.wikimedia.org/wikipedia/commons/1/12/Lo
me_Fetish_Market.jpg

http://4.bp.blogspot.com/-
Q2727TGQsLA/VH5szLYxPOI/AAAAAAAAqE0/vvqs1uZ
lGpo/s1600/sedlec.jpg

Bhangart Fort, India

http://upload.wikimedia.org/wikipedia/commons/a/a6/Bha
ngarh_fort.jpg

http://www.ermaktravel.org/Asia/India/bhangarh/New%2
0folder/3784882615_2b03cfd678%5B1%5D.jpg

Unit 731, China

http://www.unit731.org/images/Unit_731_Complex.jpg

http://upload.wikimedia.org/wikipedia/commons/4/44/Unit
_731_victim.jpg

About the Author

Conrad Bauer is passionate about everything paranormal, mysterious, and terrifying. It comes from his childhood and the famous stories his grandfather used to tell the family during summer vacation camping trips. He vividly remembers his grandfather sitting around the fire with new stories to tell everyone who would gather around and listen. His favorites were about the paranormal, including ghost stories, haunted houses, strange places, and paranormal occurrences.

Bauer is an adventurous traveller who has gone to many places in search of the unexplained and paranormal. He has been researching the paranormal and what scares people for more than four decades. He has accumulated a solid expertise and knowledge that he now shares through his books with his readers and followers.

Conrad, now retired, lives in the countryside in Ireland with his wife and two dogs.

More books from Conrad Bauer

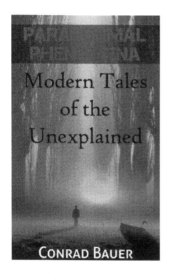

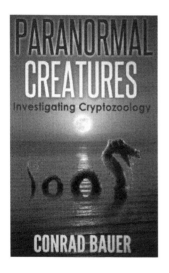

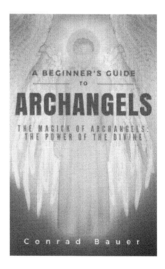

Made in the USA
San Bernardino, CA
18 June 2016